Faces of Wales

By Ann Sumner

With contributions by Louisa Briggs, Bryony Dawkes, Oliver Fairclough, Beth McIntyre and Charlotte Topsfield

National Museum Wales Books

2006

First published in 2006 by
Amgueddfa Cymru - National Museum Wales, Cathays Park, Cardiff, CF10 3NP, Wales.

ISBN 0 7200 0572 8

Editing and production: Mari Gordon
Design: A1 Design, Cardiff
Printed by: Zenith Media

www.museumwales.ac.uk/en/books

Acknowledgements

It has been a pleasure to work once more with AXA Art Insurance Ltd, the generous supporters of this book. I would like to thank Adam Golder, Helen George and Frances Fogel at AXA Art for their enthusiasm and dedication. Thanks are also due to my colleagues Louisa Briggs, Bryony Dawkes, Oliver Fairclough, Beth McIntyre and Charlotte Topsfield for contributing entries, as well as to Mari Gordon, Clare Smith and Penny Smith.

Ann Sumner, Head of Fine Art, Amgueddfa Cymru-National Museum Wales

Sponsor's Foreword

As specialist insurers of art and antiques, AXA Art is delighted to support this rich exploration of Welsh portraiture. The book is a true celebration of Welsh society, culture and art - there is a face to inspire everyone.

The book also includes the two new commissions AXA Art sponsored for the *Faces of Wales* exhibition (Bodelwyddan Castle, 8 October 2005 - 12 February 2006 and National Museum Cardiff, 3 June - 24 September 2006). The reception to these works was so positive that the commission is now annual, which will build the National Museum's collection of 'Welsh faces' for future generations.

Adam Golder, Chief Executive, AXA Art Insurance Limited

Introduction

This selection of works from the National Museum of Wales's collection reflects the development of portraiture from the sixteenth to the twenty-first century. It illustrates a variety of diverse faces that have contributed over the centuries to the cultural, political and economic life of Wales. The pictures range from commissioned portraits intended for public consumption or as statements of social status, to personal observations, caricatures and informal photographs. Many of the sitters are established Welsh figures, while others have strong Welsh associations. Some are internationally famous people whose Welsh ancestry is little known.

In the sixteenth, seventeenth and eighteenth centuries, it was undoubtedly the powerful elite, the country's landowners and merchants, who could afford to commission portraits.

There were, however, specific groups whose likenesses were regularly recorded over the years - among them churchmen, writers, musicians, artists and actors. For instance, the earliest clergyman to be represented here is the Reverend John Owen, the great Puritan divine who was painted in 1668; while one of the 2005 AXA Art photographic portrait commissions was of Dr Rowan Williams, formerly Archbishop of Wales and currently Archbishop of Canterbury. The earliest representation of a literary figure is the 1631 bronze bust of Edward Herbert, 1st Baron Herbert of Cherbury, who wrote what was probably the first secular autobiography in English, while the other 2005 AXA Art commission was of the highly successful author Sarah Waters, whose first novel *Tipping the Velvet* was published in 1998. While some categories of sitter might not have altered, styles of portraiture and the mediums used by artists have, inevitably, been transformed.

In the early sixteenth century, the population of Wales was only

about 350,000 and this was mostly made up of poor subsistence farmers living in Welsh-speaking rural communities. The first of the Tudor monarchs, Henry VII, was born at Pembroke Castle and his accession to the throne was welcomed in Wales. The wealthier gentry prospered during the sixteenth century, following the imposition of The Acts of Union by Henry VIII. Amongst these were the Herberts, the Mansels, the Mostyns, the Bulkeleys, the Morgans of Tredegar and the Wynns of Gwydir. They developed their estates, controlled the administration of justice and made prudent marriage alliances. Unlike Scotland or Ireland, Wales had no large urban centres before the mid-eighteenth century and no capital city for their administration, so the Welsh elite often had their portraits painted abroad or in London. For example, the earliest portraits represented in the Museum's collection are the 1st Earl of Pembroke (painted around 1560-65) and Katheryn of Berain (painted in 1568), both of whom were depicted by Netherlandish artists.

In the eighteenth century, some of the major landowning families such as the Williams Wynns and the Pennants regularly patronised successful English portrait painters in London, who had by this time replaced the dominance of the Netherlandish workshops. Therefore, no native Welsh portrait school developed during this period, as it did in Scotland. Although it is true that the great Welsh eighteenth-century artist Richard Wilson began his career as a portrait painter, he later turned to landscape, which he found more profitable, and his pupil Thomas Jones followed suit. Increased wealth in the eighteenth century also encouraged Welsh sitters to have their portraits painted in the easily accessible resort cities of Chester and Bath. One Welsh artist who was highly successful as a portrait painter was John Downman (*c.*1750-1824), who came from Ruabon and enjoyed success in Cambridge, Exeter, Wrexham and London. By the end of the eighteenth century, due to the pivotal role

Wales played in the Industrial Revolution, a new group of wealthy industrialists such as Thomas Williams, the 'King of Copper', could also now afford to have their likenesses painted by the leading London artists.

In the nineteenth century, portraiture remained for the most part the domain of the well-off, but the increasing distribution of wealth among the middle classes in Wales meant that more people now had their faces recorded for posterity. Vivid images were also created of well-known preachers and poets, such as the fiery orator the Reverend Christmas Evans and Richard Llwyd, the 'Bard of Snowdon', both painted in 1835. By the mid-nineteenth century, there was enough business for the artist James Flewitt Mullock to pursue a career within the Newport area alone.

It was the development of photography that transformed the nature of portraiture in Wales and beyond in the nineteenth century. It was a cheap and comparably instantaneous way of

achieving a physical likeness that could sometimes be much more faithful than the flattery of an artist's eye. However, painted portraits continued into the twentieth century, with the production of some iconic images such as Augustus John's famous portrait of the poet Dylan Thomas and the emergence of the society portrait painter Margaret Lindsay Williams. The rich industrial history of Wales also inspired some heroic representations of workers, as well as of the mine owners themselves. For example, Evan Walters' *A Welsh Collier* of 1936, in which the sitter has only recently been identified.

Portrait sculpture has always been popular in Wales. Examples range from Le Sueur's bronze bust of Lord Herbert, commissioned during the reign of Charles I and one of the earliest bronze busts in Britain, to the Tredegar Workingmen's Institute's commission for Peter Lambda to create a bust of Aneurin Bevan in 1945. The Welsh sculptor Sir William Goscombe John, who died in 1952 after a long and

prolific international career, was a key cultural figure in Wales who played a major role in the formation of the Welsh national collection of art. Born in Cardiff, he was an invaluable member of the Museum's Council and regularly made generous donations to the Museum. He produced public statues, memorials and portrait busts, including one of Wales's most important politicians of the twentieth century, David, 1st Earl Lloyd George.

This book is devoted to Welsh portraiture in the National Museum's collection; further examples and an archive of Welsh portraiture can be seen at the National Library of Wales in Aberystwyth, which has collected portraiture since its foundation, and in the National Portrait Gallery, London.

Ann Sumner, Head of Fine Art, Amgueddfa Cymru-National Museum Wales

Adriaen van Cronenburgh (*c.*1520/25-*c.*1604)

Katheryn of Berain, 'The Mother of Wales' (1534-1591)

1568
oil on panel

Katheryn of Berain was the daughter of Tudur ap Robert Vychan of Berain in Denbighshire and the granddaughter of an illegitimate son of Henry VII. She married four times and had six children. Because she had so many children and step-children she became known as 'The Mother of Wales' and many families in north Wales could claim ancestry to her. Her first husband, John, was the son and heir of Sir John Salusbury of Llewenni. After John's death in 1556, she married Sir Richard Clough, a wealthy merchant from Denbigh who lived in Antwerp and Hamburg. He died in 1570, and she returned to Berain. She then married Morris Wynn of Gwydir, who died in 1580. Finally, in 1584, aged 50, she married Edward Thelwall of Plas-y-ward. She died seven years later and is buried at Llanefydd church, next to her first husband.

The Friesian artist van Cronenburgh probably painted this portrait while Katheryn was in the Netherlands. The skull, a common device in portraiture of the period, is symbolic of mortality.

Purchased,1957
NMW A 19

AN° DNI 1565

Netherlandish School

William Herbert, 1st Earl of Pembroke (1507-1570)

*c.*1560-65
oil on panel

William Herbert was an influential political and military figure during the reigns of Henry VIII, Edward VI and Mary I. Intensely proud of his Welsh ancestry, he owned land in south Wales and the west of England. His first wife was Anne Parr, sister of Henry VIII's last queen, and it was through her influence that he rose to power. He was one of Edward VI's twelve privy councillors and maintained his political ascendancy on the accession of Mary I in 1554, when he was appointed Captain General of forces in France.

He is shown here at the end of his long and successful military career. He is wearing distinctive Italian armour, which was probably Milanese and known as a medium cavalry 'demi-lance'. An identical suit of armour is worn by the Earl of Essex in a later portrait of 1577, suggesting that Pembroke either gave or left this suit of armour to the young courtier. The artist is unknown but almost certainly Netherlandish, given the sophisticated style in which the breeches and armour are painted.

Purchased, 2000
NMW A 16468

HONI SOIT QVI MAL Y PENSE

British School

Sir Thomas Mansel and his wife, Jane

*c.*1625
oil on canvas

The Mansels of Margam Abbey were one of the wealthiest families in south Wales. Sir Thomas (1556-1631) was MP for Glamorgan. He was prominent at the Court of James I, and purchased a baronetcy in 1611. He is shown here with his second wife, Jane.

Double portraits were common in seventeenth-century portraiture, but it is unusual to see a tender gesture such as holding hands. Lady Jane holds a marigold in her other hand, which presumably refers to their daughter Mary, who appeared with her parents in another related picture. The Mansels' clothes suggest wealth and the taste of a slightly older couple - the large, falling ruffs were more common in the previous decade. This is an accomplished portrait, probably painted in a London workshop.

Purchased,1984
NMW A 16

Cornelius Johnson (1593-1661)

Sir Thomas Hanmer (1612-1678)

1631
oil on canvas

Sir Thomas Hanmer of Bettisfield Park in Flintshire was a page and cup-bearer at the Court of Charles I, known as a man of taste and fashion, and a noted horticulturalist. He became MP for Flint in 1640, and during the Civil War he raised troops for the Royalists. In 1644, as the Royalist cause waned, he fled to France. There, he studied French gardens and in the 1650s he wrote *The Garden Book of Sir Thomas Hanmer.* He introduced a tulip now known as *Agate Hanmer* to Britain and cultivated vines at Bettisfield Park.

The artist Cornelius Johnson was born in London of Netherlandish parents and was popular at the Court of Charles I. He was renowned for his sensitive, restrained portraits. However, his career was eclipsed when Van Dyck arrived at Court in 1632. Indeed, Hanmer was also painted by Van Dyck in the late 1630s.

Purchased, 1944
NMW A 40

Sir Thos. Hanmer Bt MP
for Flintshire D1678

Hubert Le Sueur (*c*.1580-1658/68)

Edward Herbert, lst Baron Herbert of Cherbury (1581/3-1648)

1631
Bronze bust

Edward Herbert lived at Montgomery Castle, where he was born, and at Cherbury, his Shropshire manor. A celebrated philosopher, historian, swordsman, musician and equestrian, he was English ambassador to France in 1619 and 1622-4. He was a keen supporter of Charles I during the Civil War. He wrote what is perhaps the first secular autobiography in English and was probably the most portrayed man of his day outside royalty. The best-known image of him is a miniature portraying him as a melancholic knight by Isaac Oliver.

Le Sueur was born in France and undoubtedly learned the elements of Florentine Mannerist sculpture from Italians working in Paris. Herbert probably met him at the court of Louis XIII when he was ambassador in 1619. In 1625, Le Sueur introduced the art of bronze sculpture to Britain when he came to the Court of Charles I and created a famous bust of the King.

Purchased, 1990, with support from the National Art Collections Fund. Jointly owned with the National Trust, Powis Castle
NMW A 271

John Greenhill (1644-1676)

Reverend John Owen (1616-1683)

1668
oil on canvas

Born in Oxfordshire, John Owen was the grandson of Griffith Owen of Talhenbont in Llanegryn. As a leading Independent Puritan divine, he had an immense impact on generations of Welsh Calvinistic preachers. He was well known for opposing Archbishop Laud in the 1630s, and during the Civil War he became Chaplain to Oliver Cromwell. Later, he became Vice-Chancellor of Oxford University. Because he had friends at Court, he survived imprisonment during the Restoration.

The English artist John Greenhill was probably the most interesting of Sir Peter Lely's numerous pupils. This portrait is signed with Greenhill's monogram. It portrays a sturdy yet lively characterisation of this celebrated Puritan clergyman.

Purchased, 1971
NMW A 22

William Hogarth (1697-1764)

The Jones Family Conversation Piece

1730
oil on canvas

This group portrait was commissioned in 1730 by Robert Jones (1706-1742) of Fonmon Castle in Glamorganshire. The patron, standing on the right, is shown with his sisters Mary and Elizabeth and his younger brother Oliver. Their widowed mother, to the far right, is shown in dark blue with her pet spaniel. In the background, the peasant boy struggling with a monkey contrasts with the industrious harvesters working on the family estate.

Informal compositions such as this were inspired by Philip Mercier, court painter to Frederick, Prince of Wales, and became known as conversation pieces. Hogarth had begun his career apprenticed to a goldsmith, but he turned to engraving before training at St Martin's Lane Academy, where his talents as a draughtsman were recognized. This is one of his early conversation pieces, which helped make his reputation in this field before he moved on to the modern, moralistic subjects for which he is renowned.

Acquired with the assistance of the National Art Collections Fund and the National Heritage Memorial Fund, 1996
NMW A 3978

Anton Raphael Mengs (1728-1779)

Richard Wilson (1712/13-1782)

1752
oil on canvas

The son of a clergyman, the Welsh landscape painter Richard Wilson was born in Penegoes, near Machynlleth. He trained in London as a portrait painter but turned to landscapes while travelling in Italy in 1750. When he returned to London he enjoyed the patronage of the aristocracy and painted Italianate scenes, country houses, Welsh views and grand mythological scenes. His pupils included the Welsh painter Thomas Jones (1742-1803).

This portrait was painted in Rome in exchange for one of Wilson's landscapes. Wilson is in fact shown in front of a landscape on which he is working. The pose, deceptively like a self portrait, creates an air of professional pride. Wilson later sold this painting to one of his most important patrons, Sir Watkin Williams Wynn, who owned four landscapes by him.

Acquired with the assistance of the National Art Collections Fund, 1947
NMW A 113

Pompeo Batoni (1708-1787)

Sir Watkin Williams Wynn (1749-1789), Thomas Apperley (1734-1819) and Captain Edward Hamilton

1768-72
oil on canvas

Sir Watkin Williams Wynn was the largest private landowner of his day in Wales, with over 100,000 acres covering all the counties of north Wales and Shropshire. He was a great patron of music and the arts. He made a very expensive Grand Tour of France and Italy in 1768-9 accompanied by Edward Hamilton, a cavalry officer and amateur musician, and his neighbour Thomas Apperley of Plas Grono, near Wrexham.

Sir Watkin commissioned this portrait in 1768 when the party arrived in Rome. Batoni was the most celebrated painter in the city; his work was particularly appreciated by British travelers, and this is his finest 'Grand Tour' portrait. Sir Watkin stands on the left holding a crayon and a copy of a Raphael fresco. At the table, Apperley draws his patron's attention to a passage from Dante's *Divine Comedy*. Hamilton, a flute in his hand, gestures admiringly. The allegorical statue of Painting, located in the niche behind, emphasizes the three men's love of the arts.

Purchased, 1947
NMW A 78

Johann Zoffany (1733-1810)

Henry Knight of Tythegston (1738-1772)with his Children

*c.*1770
oil on canvas

Henry Knight was a Glamorgan landowner and a military man. He is shown here with his sons, Henry and Robert, and his daughter, Etheldra. His wife Catherine is not present, as the couple separated in 1769. It seems that he was intent on celebrating his new single-parenthood status, as he commissioned this work the following year. Knight became a captain in the 70th Foot in 1762. He probably also served in the 15th Light Dragoons, as his elder son is shown here trying on a helmet of that regiment, inscribed with its battle honour *Emsdorf*.

The German artist Johann Zoffany studied in Rome and moved to London in 1760, where he became one of King George III's favourite painters. This family group portrait powerfully evokes the wealth and sophistication of the south Wales gentry at that time. The seascape in the background of the picture refers to Tythegston, the family's home, which was a few miles from the coast between Bridgend and Porthcawl.

Purchased through the bequest of Miss June Tiley, with the assistance of the National Art Collections Fund and National Heritage Memorial Fund, 1999
NMW A 13702

Thomas Gainsborough (1727-1788)

Thomas Pennant (1726-1798)

1776
oil on canvas

The naturalist and topographer Thomas Pennant of Downing in Flintshire was a renowned traveller and antiquarian. He attended Queen's College, Oxford where he began his writing career, but left before finishing his degree. His publications included *A Tour in Wales* of 1778 and 1781, which encouraged interest in the topography and history of Wales. His servant was Moses Griffith, a talented amateur artist, who often recorded in pictures the places his master described. Pennant's *British Zoology* and *Arctic Zoology* brought him academic acclaim.

Thomas Gainsborough was one of the most talented portraitists of the eighteenth century. This portrait became famous, as many engravings were made of it. Gainsborough settled in London in 1774, after spending fifteen years in the society city of Bath. This picture illustrates the relaxed informality of his poses and the characteristic feathery brushwork of his early London period.

Purchased, 1953
NMW A 97

William Parry (1742-1791)

The Blind Harpist, John Parry (1710-1782)

*c.*1775-82
oil on canvas

This is a sensitive portrayal of John Parry, 'The Blind Harpist of Ruabon', painted by his son. John Parry was renowned as the 'father of modern harpists'. He was harpist to George III and to Sir Watkin Williams Wynn of Wynnstay, a wealthy landowner who owned a second version of this picture. The poet Thomas Gray said he had been inspired to write his poem *The Bard* after hearing Parry play the harp in Cambridge.

William Parry was a pupil of Joshua Reynolds and a close friend of the Welsh landscape painter Thomas Jones. He gained a reputation for small, whole-length portraits in oil and pastel. He was also patronised by Sir Watkin Williams Wynn.

Purchased, 1996
NMW A 3979

Thomas Lawrence (1769-1830)

Thomas Williams (1737-1802)

c.1792-5
oil on canvas

Thomas Williams was a leading figure in the Industrial Revolution. The son of Owen Williams of Cefn Coch, he became the outstanding entrepreneur of the copper industry in the late eighteenth century, sometimes being called 'The King of Copper'. From 1785, he was the chief agent of the Mynydd Parys mines near Amlwch in Anglesey and oversaw the extraction of huge quantities of copper as well as the establishment of numerous subsidiary smelting works and a distribution network of shipping. In 1790 he became MP for Great Marlow.

Thomas Lawrence was the leading portrait painter of the Regency period. Born in Bristol, he was an outstanding child prodigy and began his career in the society city of Bath. Largely self-taught, he was still in his early twenties when he painted this fine portrait. He shows Williams at the height of his power, and concentrates on his character, setting his features against the bright red curtain behind him. Williams hung the painting at his country seat in Berkshire.

Purchased, 1987
NMW A 451

Francesco Renaldi (1755-1798)

Thomas Jones (1742-1803) and his Family

1797
oil on canvas

The landscape painter Thomas Jones is best-known for his small-scale oil studies of buildings in Naples. Born in Radnorshire of a wealthy land-owning family, Jones was destined for the Church but instead decided to train as an artist under Richard Wilson. He enjoyed an early career painting subject pictures in extensive landscapes, such as *The Bard* of 1774. In 1776 he left for Italy, returning to London in 1784. In 1787 he inherited Pencerrig, the family estate near Builth Wells.

Here, Jones is shown at Pencerrig as the country squire, although he still has his easel and palette with him. Maria, his Danish wife, sits at her spinning wheel with their daughters Anna Maria and Elizabetha, who is playing the spinet. The figure behind is probably Jones's younger brother. Renaldi was an Italian painter of conversation pieces and history paintings. He trained at the Royal Academy Schools but returned to Italy in 1781 and subsequently worked in India. He and Jones were old friends; they had met in Naples and Renaldi visited Pencerrig in 1797. Although the scene appears to illustrate the perfect Welsh gentry family, it conceals the then scandalous fact that both daughters were illegitimate, as they were born in Italy when Maria was the artist's housekeeper.

Acquired with the assistance of the National Art Collections Fund, 1961
NMW A 92

Joseph Allen (1770-1839)

Mary Evans, Mrs Fryer Todd (1770-1843)

*c.*1798-9
oil on canvas

Mary Evans was the poet Samuel Taylor Coleridge's first love. He fell in love with her in 1791 while spending his school holidays with her family, but failed to declare his feelings. While touring Wales in 1794, shortly after Mary's engagement to Fryer Todd, he glimpsed her as she left a church in Wrexham, where she was visiting her grandmother. He later recalled, 'I turned sick and all but fainted away. Her image is in the sanctuary of my heart and never can it be torn away'. On her marriage, Coleridge dedicated his poem *The Sigh* to her.

The artist Joseph Allen trained in the Royal Academy Schools, working mostly in Liverpool and Manchester. He worked in Wrexham from 1798 to 1799, when he probably painted this portrait of Mary. He was patronised by several Welsh families including the Williams Wynns.

Purchased, 1991
NMW A 556

Thomas Barker (1769-1847) 'Barker of Bath'

Self Portrait

*c.*1800-5
oil on canvas

Thomas Barker was brought up in Pontypool, the son of a Japanware decorator. When he was sixteen, the family moved to Bath where his artistic talent was encouraged by Charles Spackman, a local patron who sent him to study in London and Italy. Barker's rustic subjects in the style of Gainsborough won him popularity and he regularly returned to Wales, where, along with his brothers, he found inspiration in the landscape. From 1791 onwards, he exhibited work regularly at the Royal Academy and elsewhere in London.

He painted three other self portraits. An early copy of this picture indicates that it originally extended to the right, to include a profile portrait of another patron, Thomas Shew of Weston-super-Mare, presumably the picture's first owner. An infra-red image taken recently clearly shows Shew in the background. This was later over-painted, and it is not clear when the painting was cut down.

Bequest of Miss Gwendoline Davies, 1952
NMW A 459

Francis Chantrey (1781-1841)

Thomas Johnes of Hafod (1748-1816)

1811
marble bust

Thomas Johnes is renowned for laying out his famous pleasure grounds at Hafod in Cardiganshire following the 'Picturesque Landscape' theories of his cousin Richard Payne Knight of Downton Castle in Herefordshire. Visitors flocked to see the spectacular paradise created in a location previously regarded as remote and inhospitable. He was a prominent agriculturalist who embarked on a major programme of agricultural improvements on his estate and founded a local society for the continuation of such improvements.

Johnes was also a patron of the arts, and he favoured the sculptor Thomas Banks. A portrait bust by Banks was lost in a fire at Hafod in 1807. This work might have been commissioned from Francis Chantrey, who was a celebrated sculptor of statues and busts, in order to replace it. Chantrey had an extremely successful career and made a fortune, which he bequeathed to the Royal Academy in London for the continued purchase of works of art 'of the highest merit'.

Purchased, 1991
NMW A 514

Martin Archer Shee (1769-1850)

Sir Thomas Picton (1758-1815)

*c.*1812-13

Sir Thomas Picton was born in Poyston, Pembrokeshire and joined the army in 1771. A life-long soldier, he saw action in the American War of Independence, served in the West Indies and became a somewhat controversial Governor of Trinidad. He made his reputation as Commander of the 3rd Division during the Peninsular War of 1809-13. Although regarded as unconventional and uncouth, Picton was one of the most talented of the senior officers working for the Duke of Wellington. He was described as a 'rough foul-mouthed devil' by Wellington, who also conceded that he 'always behaved extremely well; no man could do better in the difficult services I assigned him'. He was promoted to Lieutenant General in 1811 and showed outstanding bravery at the taking of Badajoz on the Portugese border in 1812. This portrait may have been painted in that year as he is set against a background of smoke and fire, and a building at the bottom left may represent the famous castle at Badajoz.

The Irish-born artist Shee was predominantly a portrait painter who came to London in 1788 and enrolled at the Royal Academy school in 1790. He eventually succeeded Lawrence as President of the Royal Academy in 1830 and was renowned as an energetic reformer who pioneered national support for the arts.

Transferred from the Cardiff Museum in 1912
NMW A 473

William Beechey (1753-1839)

Thomas Assheton-Smith (1752-1828)

1826
oil on canvas

Thomas Assheton-Smith of Y Faenol, near Bangor was one of the leading 'Improvers' of his generation. He enclosed his estates and rebuilt Y Faenol in a neo-classical style. He constructed roads, cottages and a harbour, and between 1809 and 1826 he developed the great Dinorwig slate quarry in Llanberis. By 1826 he employed 800 quarrymen, producing 20,000 tons of slate. He was MP for Caernarfonshire from 1775 to 1784.

As a young man he had been painted by Nathaniel Dance, but this portrait shows him in old age. It was commissioned by the Caernarfon Corporation for the Grand Jury Room at Caernarfon but it was later removed to Y Faenol. William Beechey had a long and successful career as a portraitist. He painted George III and George IV, and was made portrait painter to Queen Charlotte in 1793.

Purchased,1985
NMW A 474

William Jones (active 1818-1869)

Richard Llwyd, 'Bard of Snowdon' (1752-1835)

1835
oil on canvas

Richard Llwyd was a writer, poet and noted authority on Welsh heraldry and genealogy. He was born at the King's Head in Beaumaris, Anglesey, the son of a coastal trader. He attended Beaumaris Free School before entering domestic service. By 1770, he was steward and secretary to Griffith of Caerhun, near Conway. There he pursued his interest in books, manuscripts and records and worked with writers including Sir Richard Colt Hoare and Richard Fenton. He published *Poems, Tales, Odes and Sonnets, translations from the British* in 1804, but his best known work was *Beaumaris Bay* (1800). From 1807, he lived in Chester. He was elected an honorary member of the Cymmrodorion Society in 1824.

The artist William Jones worked in Chester. The date of this painting was only recently discovered, following surface cleaning.

Purchased, 1933
NMW A 437

William Roos (1808-1878)

Reverend Christmas Evans (1766-1838)

1835
oil on canvas

Born on Christmas Day at Esgaer-waen near Llandysul in Cardiganshire, Christmas Evans was a renowned Baptist minister and one of the most powerful preachers in Wales. He was ordained into the Baptist Church in 1789. In 1791, he took charge of the Anglesey Baptists and in 1802 he restarted the North Wales Baptist Association. A man of great physical presence - reputedly 7ft tall - he had lost an eye in a fight in his youth, and the empty socket was sewn shut. He was an evangelical 'fire-and-brimstone' revivalist, who attracted large congregations with his thundering sermons.

The artist William Roos was born at Bodgadfa in Anglesey and enjoyed local success as a portraitist and painter of animals. In this painting, his best known work, he captures the powerful physical presence of Evans.

Purchased, 1907
NMW A 2410

William Etty (1787-1849)

Louisa Rolls, Mrs Vaughan (d.1853)

*c.*1835
oil on canvas

Louisa Elizabeth Vaughan was the daughter of John Rolls of The Hendre in Monmouthshire. She married John Francis Vaughan of Courtfield in Herefordshire, a member of an old Welsh Catholic family. Their children included Cardinal Vaughan, Archbishop of Westminster, four priests and four nuns.

Born in Yorkshire, William Etty was best known for his large history scenes and his nudes. However, he also had a wide range of loyal patrons who commissioned portraits from him. He was much indebted to the Venetian Renaissance, and the fashionable 1830s clothing and hairstyle here are endowed with the colours of Titian.

Purchased, 1958
NMW A 438

James Flewitt Mullock (1818-1892)

Sir Charles Morgan (1760-1846) at the Castleton ploughing competition

1845
oil on canvas

Sir Charles Morgan of Tredegar was a scientific agricultural improver, interested in stock breeding, soil treatment, drainage and new implements and machinery; he also leased out his land for coal and iron extraction. He was President of the Royal Agricultural Society of England and established the Tredegar Cattle Show in 1819.

The artist James Flewitt Mullock, whose well-off family came from Cheshire, was born in Newport, where his father was Mayor in 1842. He was renowned for his animal and sporting paintings and small-scale portraits. From 1868 to 1877 he was listed in local directories as Newport's sole teacher of art, and it seems he never exhibited outside his home town. This picture shows the first Castleton Ploughing Match, which took place in Cae Shop Field in Castleton in January 1845. Morgan, well into his seventies by then, attended as principal supporter of the Castleton Ploughing Club along with some hundred or more spectators. Although the landscape is immediately recognizable as the Gwent levels with the Bristol Channel in the background, the picture is probably a composed record of the event painted later, rather than at the time.

Purchased, 2004
NMW A 26149

Karoly Marko the Younger (1822-1891)

Adelina Patti (1843-1919)

*c.*1873-5
oil on canvas

Adelina Patti was a famous opera singer renowned both for her soprano voice and her lively love-life. Born in Madrid and raised in New York, her debut was in Donizetti's *Lucia di Lammermoor* in 1859. In the mid-1860s she moved to London and in 1878 she purchased Craig-y-Nos, a neo-gothic castle between Ystradgynlais and Brecon, for her lover Ernest Nicolini, just as her first marriage was hitting the divorce courts. She built her own private opera house at the castle and had a railway link constructed so that she could travel to her remote home in her own luxurious carriage. She and Nicolini married in Swansea in 1886. After Nicolini's death in 1898, she married Baron Rolf Cederstrom in the Roman Catholic Church in Brecon. Her last public performance was in 1914; she died at Craig-y-Nos at the age of 76.

The Hungarian artist Karoly Marko was the son of a landscape painter. He worked in Italy with his father and then settled in Russia, where he painted Patti. She is dressed for skating in the harsh Russian winter.

Gift of M. E. Hatherill
NMW A 515

K. Marko.

Ambrose McEvoy (1878-1927)

Gwen John (1876-1939)

1901
oil on canvas

Born in Haverfordwest, Gwen John is now widely regarded as one of the most important women artists of the twentieth century. She studied at the Slade School of Art at the same time as her brother Augustus, who achieved considerable fame in his lifetime. She, however, lived for most of her life in Paris, where she had a long affair with the sculptor Rodin. In 1913, she converted to Catholicism and spent her later life in the suburban village of Meudon. Her small-scale portraits and still-lifes often reflect her search for isolation and solitude.

Ambrose McEvoy was a contemporary of John's at the Slade School of Art. Known for his flamboyant dress and attitude, McEvoy was a follower of Whistler, whose influence can be seen in the subtle, almost monochrome tones and soft lines of this painting. John and McEvoy had a relationship, which ended in 1901. However, they remained on good terms, and as well as this painting he made many drawings of her.

Purchased, 1998
NMW A 12827

George Roilos (1867-1928)

William Goscombe John (1860-1952)

1902
oil on canvas

William Goscombe John was born in Cardiff and became a prolific, highly respected sculptor who was renowned for his public statues and portrait busts. As an active member of the Welsh National Museum's Council, he did much to form the early national collections.

George Roilos was a Greek artist working in London at the turn of the nineteenth century. This is a classic depiction of the artist at work, showing the sculptor in his studio working on the Coldstream Guards South African War Memorial for St Paul's Cathedral. He stands by his easel, with a bronze on a plinth to his right to indicate his main creative medium. In 1953, Goscombe John's daughter described this picture as the 'most really sympathetic' likeness of her father.

Gift of Sir William Goscombe John, 1940
NMW A 588

Margaret Lindsay Williams (1888-1960)

Clara Novello Davies (1861-1943)

1915
oil on canvas

The Cardiff-born Dame Clara Novello Davies was named after the Italian soprano, Clara Novello. She came from a highly musical Welsh family and became a celebrated singing teacher and choral conductor. She is perhaps best-known, however, for her famous son, Ivor Novello (born David Ivor Davies). Just six months after giving birth to her son, Davies took her Welsh Ladies Choir on tour to places as far away as Chicago. She encouraged her son to also devote his life to music.

Margaret Lindsay Williams is arguably one of Wales's most important female portraitists. Also from Cardiff, Williams trained at the Royal Academy Schools in London, where she was deeply influenced by her teacher, John Singer Sargent. Her career flourished in London between the wars. She painted portraits of actors, soldiers, politicians and industrialists and received commissions to paint members of the Royal family. Ivor Novello also posed for Williams.

Gift of Madame Clara Novello Davies, 1933
NMW A 5169

Harold Knight (1874-1961)

Dame Gwen Ffrangcon-Davies (1891-1992)

1922
oil on canvas

Gwen Ffrangcon-Davies was a legend of the classical British stage during her career, which spanned 80 years. She was born in London, making her stage debut in 1911 in *A Midsummer Nights' Dream*. Her first major London success was in Rutland Boughton's *The Immortal Hour* in 1922. This portrait shows her as the lost Princess Etain in that production. In 1924, she acted alongside John Gielgud in *Romeo and Juliet*. They are generally regarded as being the century's greatest performers in those roles.

Harold Knight was born in Nottingham and trained in London and Paris. In 1903, he married the painter Laura Johnson. The Knights lived for some years in Holland and later moved to Cornwall, where they became influential figures within the Newlyn School, a thriving artistic community who lived and painted on the western Cornish coast. This portrait dates from after their return to settle in London in 1918.

Purchased, 1924.
NMW A 592

Desmond Chute (1896-1962)

David Jones (1895-1974)

1926
pencil on paper

David Jones was arguably one of the twentieth century's most important modernist artists and poets. His complex and intricate work was inspired by his service in the First World War as a Private in the Royal Welch Fusiliers, as well his conversion to the Roman Catholic faith and his Welsh heritage. Soon after being received into the Catholic Church in 1921, he joined Eric Gill in Ditchling in Sussex and became a member of the Guild of Third Order of St Joseph and St Dominic.

It was there that he met Desmond Chute, one of the Guild's founders, who taught Jones wood engraving. Jones went on to become one of the finest British engravers of the twentieth century. Chute has captured Jones here in a very simple yet striking pencil portrait.

Purchased, 1939
NMW A 16813

David Jones
Chute 1926

John Lavery (1856-1941)

David, lst Earl Lloyd George (1863-1945)

oil on canvas
1935

David Lloyd George, the 'Welsh Wizard' of early twentieth-century politics, was a member of Asquith's reforming Liberal government and Chancellor of the Exchequer in 1908. During the First World War he was Minister of Munitions, becoming Prime Minister in the Coalition Government from 1916 to 1922. His greatest political achievement was probably the 1911 National Insurance Act. Augustus John and Christopher Williams also painted him.

Born in Belfast, John Lavery trained in Glasgow and Paris before settling in London. There, as a society painter, he was a rival to Augustus John in their early careers.

Gift of Sir John Lavery, 1938
NMW A 2955

Evan Walters (1893-1951)

A Welsh Collier

1936
oil on canvas

Many portraits and images of miners exist in Wales's national collection, as the rich mining history of south Wales has been well documented. Until recently, the identity of this collier was unknown. His family have now identified him as Thomas Rees from Llangyfelach near Swansea. The scar on his forehead was caused by a pit accident.

Evan Walters was a prolific and innovative Welsh artist. He experimented with colour and vision, as we can see in this painting. This is one of two pictures Walters painted of Rees, who was his distant cousin.

Bequest of Evan Walters, 1953
NMW A 2149

WALTERS
1936

Augustus John (1878-1961)

Dylan Thomas (1914-1953)

*c.*1937
oil on canvas

Augustus John met Dylan Thomas at the Fitzroy Tavern, Soho, probably in 1935, where he introduced him to Caitlin Macnamara, whom Thomas married in 1937. John painted the young poet twice, probably in late 1937 or early 1938, when Thomas and Caitlin were staying at her mother's house not far from John's home at Fryern Court.

Augustus John was one of the stars of the Slade School of Art, where he trained with his sister Gwen. He was a highly accomplished draughtsman and enjoyed considerable success as a society portrait painter. This is a classic example of portraiture by John, brightly coloured and with lively brushwork. The artist recalled 'I got him to sit for me twice, the second portrait being the more successful: provided with a bottle of beer he sat very patiently.'

Gift of Contemporary Art Society, 1942
NMW A 159

Lucian Freud (b.1922)

Cedric Morris (1889-1982)

1940
oil on canvas

The artist Cedric Morris ran the East Anglian School of Painting and Drawing, first in Dedham then in Benton End, where Freud began studying in 1939. He was born in Sketty, and studied in Paris before establishing the School with his partner, Arthur Lett-Haines.

Morris was undoubtedly a most significant influence on Lucian Freud's early work. In 1981, Freud said 'Cedric taught me to paint and more important to keep at it. He did not say much, but let me watch him at work. I have always admired his paintings and everything about him.' Morris returned the favour by painting his young pupil in 1941, a work which is now in the Tate Gallery collection.

Acquired with the assistance of the Derek Williams Trust and HM Government Acceptance-in-Lieu, 1998
NMW A 12875

Peter Lambda (1911-1995)

Aneurin Bevan (1897-1960)

1945
bronze

Aneurin or 'Nye' Bevan was born in Tredegar, the son of a miner. A Trade Union leader and MP for Ebbw Vale from 1929, and a key member of the post-war Labour government, he was a staunch believer in equality through state intervention. Bevan's greatest achievement was arguably establishing the National Health Service in 1948 when he was Minister of Health in Clement Atlee's government. In 1959, Bevan became Deputy Leader of the Labour Party, despite having been diagnosed with cancer.

Peter Lambda was a writer and sculptor who was born in Budapest in Hungary. He originally studied medicine before turning his attention to sculpture. He moved to London in 1938. He met Nye Bevan in 1945, and this paved the way for one of his most successful portrait heads. It was commissioned for the Workingmen's Institute in Tredegar.

Purchased, 1973
NMW A 2520

Heloise Crista (b.1926)

Frank Lloyd Wright (1867-1959)

1956
bronze bust

Born in Wisconsin of Welsh descent, Frank Lloyd Wright is considered to be one of the founding fathers of modern architecture. He first came to prominence with his 'Prairie Style', which had characteristic low horizontal lines and open interior spaces. Wright believed in organic architecture, 'a free architecture. Architecture that belongs where you see it standing - and is a grace to the landscape instead of a disgrace'. His designs gradually became more abstract and geometric and he began to use cast blocks of concrete. His last architectural project was the iconic Guggenheim Museum in Manhattan, a large concrete spiral. His innovative work, which spanned seven decades, influenced several generations of architects.

Heloise Crista studied Applied Art at the University of California, during which time she discovered the writings of Frank Lloyd Wright. In 1949 she became an apprentice at Wright's School of Architecture at Taliesin in Wisconsin, where she modelled this work, a commission from the architect's wife.

Gift of Wallace Harrison, Philip Johnson, John Maclane Johansen, Edward Durel Stone and Fred Madox, 1969
NMW A 314

Ronald Moody (1900-1984)

Paul Robeson (1898-1976)

1968
bronze

Paul Robeson was an American actor, singer and civil rights activist. He felt a strong affinity with Wales and was particularly impressed by the sense of community he experienced amongst the south Wales miners. He toured south Wales in the 1930s, performing at concerts in Aberdare and Mountain Ash. In 1941, he starred in *The Proud Valley*, a film in which he played a stoker in a Welsh coal town. Although refused a passport during the McCarthy era, Robeson addressed the 1957 Miners' Eisteddfod in Porthcawl via the new transatlantic telephonic link.

The sculptor and writer Ronald Moody was born in Jamaica, moving to England in 1923 to study dentistry. He was profoundly affected by Egyptian sculpture at the British Museum, which inspired him to change career. This portrait was commissioned by the DDR Akademie der Kunst in Berlin, but political considerations forced them to abandon the commission. Despite Robeson's unpredictability as a sitter, Moody managed to complete the sculpture for the 1968 Human Rights exhibition.

Gift of Cynthia Moody, 2004
NMW A 26343

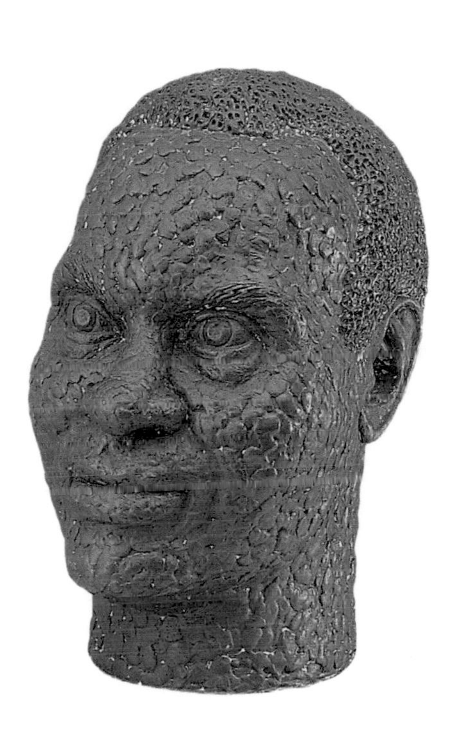

David Hurn (b.1934)

Tanni Grey (b.1969)

1996
gelatin silver print

The paralympic champion Dame Tanni Grey-Thompson was born in Cardiff. A wheelchair user since the age of seven, she has become one of the most respected athletes in Britain. Her highly successful paralympic career began in Seoul in 1988, since which time she has won eleven gold medals and six London Marathons. She was made a Dame in the 2005 New Years Honours list.

David Hurn is a renowned photojournalist who was partly brought up in Wales and has a long affinity with the country and its people. This image is one from a series of portraits of people who Hurn says 'have enriched my life and that of Wales.'

Purchased, 1999
NMW A 13350

QUICKIE
QUICKIE

David Hurn (b.1934)

R. S. Thomas (1913-2001)

1997
duotone photographic print

Ronald Stuart Thomas was one of the most significant poets of the twentieth century. He was ordained a priest of the Anglican Church in Wales in 1937, and published his first volume of poetry, *The Stones of the Field*, in 1946. Although he wrote in English, he was a fervent supporter of Welsh nationalism, lamenting the apparent failure of Wales to resist English influence. He wrote of 'worrying continually for a dying nation ... tortured by the unanswerable question: is she being killed or does she *choose* to die? A mixture of both I'd imagine'.

This image by David Hurn portrays Thomas as hard and uncompromising, but the effect is softened by the rose he holds. It is an insightful portrait of an individual who was often described as a man of contradictions.

Purchased, 1999
NMW A 13359

Nicholas Sinclair (b.1954)

Kyffin Williams (b.1918)

black and white photograph

Kyffin Williams is one of Wales's most celebrated living artists. He was born in Llangefni in Anglesey and only took up painting after being invalided out of the Royal Welch Fusiliers on account of epilepsy. He studied at the Slade School in London from 1941 to 1944 and went on to become the Senior Art Master at Highgate School. Williams has received many rewards and accolades including holding the post of President of the Royal Cambrian Academy from 1969 to 1976 and again from 1992. He was made a Royal Academician in 1974. In 1991 he received the Medal of the Honourable Society of Cymmrodorion and in 1995 the Glyndŵr medal and the Medal of the Contemporary Art Society of Wales. He was given an OBE in 1974 and he was knighted in 1999.

Nicholas Sinclair was born in London in 1954. His work has been widely exhibited and published in Britain, Europe and the USA. He was made a Hasselblad Master in 2003. This photograph is from a portfolio of twelve works taken between 1987 and 2003.

Purchased, 2004
NMW A 27066

Ric Bower (b.1968)

Sarah Waters (b.1966)

2005
digital c-type print

The writer Sarah Waters was born in Neyland, Pembrokeshire. She completed her first novel, *Tipping the Velvet*, in 1998. Waters has written three further novels, *Affinity* (1999), *Fingersmith* (2002) and *The Night Watch* (2006), and has won numerous awards, including Author of the Year at the 2003 British Book Awards. Both *Tipping the Velvet* and *Fingersmith* have been adapted for BBC television drama series.

Ric Bower was born in London and now lives and works in west Wales. He studied Fine Art in Manchester, and in 2005 gained a first class honours degree in Photography from Coleg Sir Gâr, Carmarthenshire. Previous exhibitions include a solo show in 2001 at the Emrys Gallery in Haverfordwest. An established portrait painter, he has more recently engaged in photographic practice, and was one of the finalists in the Schweppes 2005 Photographic Portrait Prize. Bower's photographic process is very much influenced by historic painting, using rich colour and symbolism to create a highly charged environment, as illustrated by this portrait.

Acquired through the AXA Art Photographic Portrait Commission, 2005
NMW A 27902

Dominic Hawgood (b.1980)

Dr Rowan Williams, Archbishop of Canterbury (b.1950)

2005
digital c-type print

Rowan Williams was born in Swansea. After studying Theology at Cambridge, he began his career as an academic and was made a Professor at Oxford University in 1986. He became Bishop of Monmouth in 1992 and Archbishop of Wales in 2000, before being consecrated Archbishop of Canterbury in 2002. A renowned thinker and theologian, he has published numerous books, including two volumes of poetry.

Dominic Hawgood grew up in Shropshire and graduated in 2005 from University of Wales, Newport with first class honours in Photographic Art. During his studies he exhibited in numerous group shows, and in April 2005 was a finalist in the first annual *Bright Young Things* exhibition in Berlin. Hawgood says of this project 'This commission, my first, is a signifier of my drive to inject my practice with a new professional relevance, and to apply my skills in new ways'. Hawgood has created a reflective, atmospheric image, reminiscent of the paintings of Vermeer in its use of interior space and contrasts of light and dark.

Acquired through the AXA Art Photographic Portrait Commission, 2005
NMW A 27901